THE SCOTTISH KITCHEN
Recipes from Scotland

D1826099

by Sue McDougall

Sphere Books Ltd., 30-32 Gray's Inn Road, London WC1X 8JL

First published 1976
First published in this edition 1983

*Use plain flour unless otherwise stated, castor sugar is
recommended for butter and sugar creamed mixtures.*

Printed and bound in Great Britain by Collins, Glasgow

SALMON SOUP

1 small fresh salmon	1 piece of celery	1 tablespoon chopped parsley
1 carrot	1 medium-sized potato	1 tablespoon brown breadcrumbs
1 turnip	Fish bones	Salt and pepper
1 onion	2 pints water	

Peel and dice the carrot and turnip. Skin and dice the onion. Wash the celery and break into small pieces. Place the vegetables and fish bones in a fish kettle or large saucepan and cover with water. Season lightly. Cover and simmer for about an hour. Strain. Peel and boil the potato in salted water. Mash the potato and use to thicken the fish stock. Clean and cut up the salmon into thin cutlets. Add to the stock and simmer gently until the salmon is cooked. Garnish with brown breadcrumbs and parsley.

CULLEN SKINK

1 Finnan-haddie
1 small onion
1 oz. butter
1 medium-sized potato
1 pint milk
Salt and pepper

Skin and wash the fish. Place in a pan or saucepan and cover with water. Skin and slice the onion. Add to the fish. Season and simmer gently until the fish is cooked. Remove the flesh of the fish and flake. Return the fish bones to the stock in the pan and cook slowly for about an hour. Peel and boil the potato in salted water. Mash with the butter. Strain the fish stock, and add the milk and flaked fish. Thicken with a little of the potato.

SCOTCH SOUP

1 lb. neck of mutton or lean stewing beef
2 carrots
1 small turnip
1 parsnip
1 medium-sized onion

1 oz. pearl barley
2 oz. shelled or frozen peas
4 tablespoons chopped kail
3 pints water
Salt and pepper

Cut up the meat and remove as much fat as possible. Wash the barley. Place the meat, and any bones, with the barley in a large saucepan. Cover with water and bring to the boil. Skim. Peel and dice the carrots, turnip and parsnip. Skin and slice the onion. Add all the vegetables, except the kail, to the saucepan. Season to taste and simmer for four hours. Remove any fat from the surface and add the chopped kail. Cook for ten minutes. Serve hot.

Cock a Leekie

A 4-5 lb. boiling fowl
8 leeks
4 pints water
giblets

3 rashers bacon
Salt and pepper
10 prunes (optional)

Pinch of parsley
Pinch of thyme
1 bayleaf

If prunes are used soak them overnight. Clean the bird and place in a large saucepan. Wash the giblets and cut up the bacon. Add to the pan. Wash the leeks and discard the coarser outer leaves. Cut the leeks into small pieces and add to the pan. Pour in water to just cover the bird and season. Bring to the boil and skim. Season with the herbs.Salt and pepper. Cover and simmer for 3½ hours until the bird is tender. Stone and halve the prunes if used. Add to the soup. Simmer for a further 30 minutes. Remove the chicken and giblets and cut into large pieces. Place in individual soup bowls. Pour the soup over the chicken and garnish with parsley.

SOUSED HERRING

4 herrings
1 bay leaf
1 blade mace

10 black peppercorns
1 small onion
¼ teaspoon salt

¼ pint vinegar
¼ pint water
Few green and red cocktail onions

Skin and cut the onion into rings. Clean and scale the fish. Split each herring along the underside. Open and ease out the backbone and as many small bones as possible. Wash and dry. Season and place a small piece of bay leaf and onion ring on each fish. Roll up from head to tail with the skin outside and secure with a cocktail stick. Place in an ovenproof dish. Cover with the vinegar and water and add the spices. Bake in the centre of a moderate oven (350°F. 177°C. gas mark 4) for 45 minutes. When cold, serve in the liquid garnished with green and red cocktail onions.

BURN TROUT — GRILLED

4 trout
Butter
2 lemons
Parsley
Salt and pepper

Clean the fish and make three diagonal cuts in each. Season and brush with melted butter. Cook under a moderate grill for 10-12 minutes, turning the fish once. Garnish with slices of lemon and parsley.

BURN TROUT — POACHED

Court Bouillion:
1½ pints water
1 tablespoon lemon juice
1 teaspoon salt
½ bay leaf
1 sprig parsley
Small piece blade mace
6 peppercorns

2 teaspoons diced onion
2 teaspoons diced carrot
2 tablespoons tarragon vinegar
2 tablespoons white wine

The Fish:
4 trout

Boil all the ingredients for the court bouillion in an enamel saucepan and simmer for 20 minutes. Strain. Clean the fish and place in a shallow dish. Cover with the court bouillion and simmer for 10-15 minutes. Serve with potatoes baked in their jackets.

ROAST GAME

2 birds
4 rashers of fatty bacon
2 rounds of bread
2 oz. butter

2 croûtes of toast
Flour
Salt and pepper

Wash and dry the birds, use the giblets for stock. Put a nub of seasoned butter inside each bird. Truss. Cover the breasts with the bacon and place on the bread in a roasting tin. Melt the butter and spoon over the birds. Bake in the centre of a very oven (450°F. 232°C.gas mark 8) for 10 minutes then in a slightly cooler oven (400°F. 204°C. gas mark 6) for a further 20-30 minutes. Baste frequently. 5 minutes before the end of the cooking time, froth the breasts to crisp the skin. This is done by removing the bacon, basting the breasts and dredging with flour. Return to a very hot oven

(450°F. 232°C. gas mark 8) until brown and frothy. Serve on croûtes of toast with clear, thin gravy, bread sauce (see page 16), game chips and a green salad.

The Gravy;
Giblets
1 dessertspoon flour
Sediment in roasting tin

The Gravy: Wash the giblets and remove any fat. Check that the greenish gall bladder is also removed. Cover the giblets with cold water. Season and simmer for 1 hour until tender. Pour off the fat from the meat tin and work 1 dessertspoonful of flour into the sediment. Strain the giblet stock and add to the roasting tin. Mix well and season. Brown if necessary and bring to the boil.

CASSEROLE GAME

2 birds
6 small onions
2 oz. button mushrooms
1 oz. butter
1 tablespoonful flour
2 tablespoonfuls sugar
Salt and pepper

The Marinade

¼ pint Burgundy
1 tablespoonful salad oil
3 shallots
4 black peppercorns
Sprig of fresh thyme
and marjoram
2 bay leaves
Slice of lemon

To Marinade: Slice the shallots and place all the ingredients for the marinade in an enamelled pan and bring to the boil. Cool. Wash and dry the birds. Truss. Pour the cold marinade over the birds and leave to soak overnight turning once or twice.

To Braise: Skin the onions and boil in salted water until tender. Drain. Melt ½ oz. of butter and add with the sugar to the onion. Stir and cook until the onions begin to colour. Place the birds and the onions in an ovenproof dish. Melt ½ oz. of butter in a pan and sauté the mushroom caps. Add to the casserole. Work the flour into the juices in the pan and gradually stir in the wine marinade. Season to taste and simmer gently to thicken. Strain over the birds. Add the mushroom stalks. Cover and cook in the centre of a moderate oven (350°F. 177°C. gas mark 4) for ½-1 hour until the birds are tender. Serve with jacket potatoes, green salad and rowan jelly.

BRAISED RED DEER

2 lb. haunch of venison
1 oz. dripping
1 onion
1 medium-sized carrot
4 sticks celery
1 orange
½ pint stock
1 tablespoon redcurrant jelly
1 teaspoon salt
½ oz. flour
½ oz. butter

The Marinade :
¼ pint red wine
1 tablespoon olive oil
1 onion
1 bay leaf
4 black peppercorns

To Marinade: Put all the ingredients of the marinade into a large pan and bring to the boil. Cool. Wash the venison and place in a large dish. Cover with the cold marinade. Leave for 24 hours, turning the meat occasionally. Drain and dry.

To Braise: Melt the dripping in an ovenproof dish and brown the meat on all sides. Remove from the dish. Skin and dice the onion. Peel the orange. Peel and dice the carrot. Cut up the celery. Place the prepared vegetables, with strips of orange peel, into the dish. Cover and cook gently for 5-10 minutes until the onion is soft. Strain the marinade liquor into the dish and add the stock. Place the venison on top of the vegetables. Season. Cover and cook slowly for 2-2½ hours until the meat is tender. Remove the meat and vegetables and keep hot in a large dish. Decant the liquor into a pan, add the orange juice and red currant jelly. Work the ½ oz. flour and ½ oz. butter together to form kneaded butter. Bring the liquid in the pan to the boil and add the kneaded butter in small pieces to thicken it.

BREAD SAUCE

3 oz. white breadcrumbs
1 oz. butter
1 medium-sized onion
2 cloves
¾ pint milk
Salt and pepper

Skin the onion and press the cloves into it. Place in a saucepan with the milk and breadcrumbs. Season. Cover and leave to stand in a warm place for 1 hour. Then simmer gently for 5 minutes taking care not to burn the sauce. Remove the onion and stir in the butter. Keep hot in a covered dish.

GILLIES VENISON

2 lb. venison
2 oz. flour
2 oz. bacon fat
2 rashers streaky bacon
1 onion

1 pint stock
2 tablespoons port wine
Salt and pepper
Seasoned flour

Cut the meat into 1 inch cubes and dip in seasoned flour. Melt the fat to a depth of 2 inches in a casserole. Skin and slice the onion and heat gently until it begins to colour. Add the pieces of venison and turn gently until they brown. Chop the bacon and add to the casserole. Season. Cover and cook for 1 hour until the meat is tender. Drain the meat on to absorbent kitchen paper. Decant excess fat from the pan. Stir the flour into the remaining sediment. Stir in the stock and pour in the port wine. Serve with mashed potatoes and green vegetables.

A STOVED HOWTOWDIE WI' DRAPPIT EGGS

A 3-4 lb. roasting chicken
2 lb. spinach
6 small onions or shallots
4 oz. butter
2 cloves
4 black peppercorns
Pinch mace
1 pint stock — from giblets
2 tablespoons cream
Salt and pepper

The Stuffing
2 oz. breadcrumbs
1 small shallot — finely chopped
1 teaspoon chopped tarragon
1 teaspoon chopped parsley
2 tablespoons milk
Salt and pepper

The Stuffing: Moisten the breadcrumbs with milk and add the chopped shallot, tarragon and parsley. Season.

The Bird: Wash and clean the chicken. Put the stuffing in the bird. Melt half the butter in a casserole and lightly brown the onions. Place the chicken in the middle of the dish and cook for 20 minutes in a hot oven (400°F. 204°C. gas mark 6). Add the herbs, seasoning and stock. Cover and cook for 1-1½ hours at 350°F 177°C gas mark 4 until the bird is tender. Cook the spinach separately, drain and keep hot. Remove the bird on to a hot platter and pour the stock into a saucepan. Poach 4 eggs in this stock. Place the spinach around the chicken and place the eggs on the spinach. Chop the liver and add to the stock. Simmer for 5-10 minutes. Mash the liver to thicken the stock. Remove from the heat and add the cream and butter cut into small pieces. Re-heat but do not boil. Pour the sauce over the chicken but not over the spinach.

SCOTS BRAWN

½ ox head
1 ox foot
½ teaspoon mustard
1 bay leaf

1 blade mace
Pinch cayenne
½ teaspoon allspice, nutmeg or cloves
Salt and pepper

Soak the half oxhead and the foot in cold water for 2-3 hours. Break into several pieces. Remove as much fat and marrow as possible from the foot. Scald the head and foot with boiling water, scrape and clean. Place the half ox head and the foot in a large saucepan and cover with cold water. Add two tablespoonfuls salt. Bring to the boil. Skim carefully and simmer for 3 hours. Then remove the head and foot and cut away all the meat from them. Return the bones to the water and add water, if necessary, to cover them. Add the bay leaf and mace. Simmer for 3 hours and strain.

When cold, this will form a jelly. Remove all the fat from the top of this jelly. Put the meat with the jelly/stock into a saucepan and simmer for 20 minutes. Add the mustard and allspice or nutmeg or cloves. Season with pepper and a pinch of cayenne. Pour into wet moulds and leave in a cool place to set. Serve with green salad.

HAGGIS

The large stomach bag of a sheep
The pluck including the heart, liver and lights
8 oz. beef suet
4 oz. coarse oatmeal

3 medium-sized onions
Pinch cayenne
Salt and black pepper

Toast the oatmeal until brown. Clean the bag thoroughly. Wash it in cold water and turn inside out and scrape it with a knife. Soak overnight in cold salted water. Wash the pluck well. Put in a large saucepan, cover with cold water and bring to the boil. Leave the wind pipe hang over the side of the saucepan to let out any inpurities. Change the water after 5 minutes. Boil for 1½ hours. Remove from the saucepan and cut away any pipes and gristle. Mince the heart, lights and beef suet together. Grate half the liver and add to the meat mixture. Skin and finely chop the onions and add with the oatmeal. Season with salt and pepper and a pinch of cayenne if liked. When cold, add enough of the liquid that the pluck was boiled in beef stock) to make a mixture with a soft dropping consistency. Fill the stomach so that it is just over half full leaving plenty of room for the mixture to swell. Sew the bag securely and boil slowly for 3 hours in the remaining stock from the pluck. Top up with water as necessary to keep the haggis covered. As soon as the bag begins to swell, prick it all over with a large needle to prevent it bursting. Serve very hot with mashed potatoes and turnips.

POT HAGGIS

8 oz. liver	1 medium-sized onion
2 oz. beef suet	½ pint beef stock
3 oz. coarse oatmeal	Salt and pepper

Cut up the liver and skin and slice the onion. Simmer in salted water for 30-40 minutes until the meat is tender. When cool, mince the meat. Heat the oatmeal gently in a thick frying pan until it browns. Shred the suet. Mix the suet, meat, onion and oatmeal together. Add enough liquor from the meat to give the mixture a soft dropping consistency. Season to taste. Place in a greased pudding basin and close with foil. Steam for 2 hours. Serve with mashed potatoes and turnips.

BLACK PUDDING

2 pints pig's or ox blood	*1 lb. suet*	*8 oz. onions*
½ pint milk	*3 oz. oatmeal*	*Salt and pepper*

Wash the pudding skins thoroughly and soak overnight in salted water. When the blood is cold, add 1 teaspoon salt. Pass through a hair sieve. Stir in the milk and shredded suet and oatmeal. Skin and dice the onions and add to the mixture. Season to taste.

To fill a pudding, skin, tie at one end and turn inside out. When filled tie off in equal lengths. Place in water that is just off the boil. After 5 minutes, prick all over with a large needle. Boil for half an hour. When cooked remove from the water and hang in a cool place to dry. To serve, re-heat in boiling water for 10-15 minutes.

HIGHLAND BEEF BALLS

1 lb. beef steak
½ lb. suet
½ teaspoon saltpetre
½ teaspoon sugar
½ teaspoon ground ginger
¼ teaspoon ground cloves
Salt and black pepper
Fat for frying

Mince the beef steak and suet and mix all the ingredients together, except a little of the suet. Melt the suet kept back. Form the meat mixture into small balls and cover with a little melted suet. Fry in deep fat.

MINCE COLLOPS

1 lb. steak	1 medium-sized onion
1 oz. suet	½ pint beef stock
1 oz. oatmeal	Dash of mushroom ketchup or Worcester sauce
½ oz. cooking fat	Salt and pepper

Melt the fat in a frying pan. Skin and cut up the onion. Fry the onion gently until it starts to colour. Mince the steak and shred the suet and add to the pan. Stir with a wooden spoon so as to separate the pieces of meat. Heat until the meat begins to brown. Stir in the oatmeal and enough stock to just cover the meat mixture. Season and flavour to taste adding mushroom ketchup or Worcester sauce if liked. Simmer for 45 minutes to 1 hour. Serve on toast topped by poached eggs.

INKY-PINKY

Cold roast beef
Boiled carrots
1 onion
Beef stock
1 oz. flour
½ oz. beef fat
Salt and pepper

Melt the fat in a pan. Skin and slice the onions. Heat gently in the pan until it begins to colour. Remove the onion and work in the flour using a wooden spoon. Stir in the stock to make a brown gravy. Slice the beef and carrots and place in a deep pan with the onion. Cover with the gravy and simmer until heated thoroughly. Serve hot with boiled potatoes.

SCOTS EGGS

5 eggs
8 oz. pork sausage meat
1 teaspoon mixed herbs
1 tablespoon finely chopped parsley

2 oz. browned breadcrumbs
1 tablespoon flour
Fat for frying
Salt and pepper

Hard boil 4 of the eggs for 10 minutes. Pour off the hot water and fill the pan with cold water When they are cooled, shell the eggs. Season the flour and dust the eggs with it. Mix the herbs and parsley into the sausage meat and divide it into four. Cover each egg with sausage meat. Lightly beat the uncooked egg. Brush the Scots egg with the beaten egg and roll in breadcrumbs. Fry the eggs in deep fat turning occasionally until golden brown. Drain on absorbent kitchen paper.

COLCANNON

1 medium-sized cabbage
1 lb. potatoes
1 lb. turnips
1 lb. carrots
½ oz. butter
Salt and pepper
Brown sauce

Clean and boil the cabbage in salted water.
and boil the potatoes, turnips and carrots in sal
water. Drain the cabbage and shred finely. Drain
the vegetables and mash. Melt the butter in a pan
and add all the vegetables. Mix together. Season to
taste and add a little brown sauce. Serve hot with
cold meats.

SKIRLIE

4 oz. oatmeal
2 oz. dripping or suet
1 onion
Salt and pepper

Melt the fat. Skin and dice the onion and fry
lightly in the fat. Stir in the oatmeal to make a
thick mixture. Season to taste and cook for a few
minutes. Serve hot with mashed potatoes, turnips
or boiled cabbage.

HIGHLAND CRUDDY BUTTER OR CROWDIE

2 pints fresh or sour milk
½ teaspoon rennet
1 tablespoon cream
Salt and pepper

Gently warm the milk until it is tepid. Stir in the rennet and leave to stand in a warm place until a curd is formed. Cut into 1 inch cubes and leave to stand for 10 minutes for the whey to separate. Run off as much whey as possible and tie the curds in muslin. When dry, stir in the cream and season to taste. Pack into a mould. Herbs or chopped almonds or walnuts may also be added.

SCOTS SEED CAKE

8 oz. flour
1 teaspoon baking powder
6 oz. butter
6 oz. castor sugar

1 oz. caraway seeds
3 oz. mixed peel
3 eggs

Grease a 6-inch cake tin and line with greased greaseproof paper. Cream the butter and sugar until the mixture is white and fluffy. Beat in the eggs, one at a time, adding a little flour to prevent curdling. Sift the baking powder and flour together. Stir the caraway seeds and mixed peel into the flour. Fold the flour mixture into the fat and sugar. Turn into the cake tin and level the top. Cook at the bottom of a moderate oven (350°F. 177°C. gas mark 4) for 1½ hours until the cake is well risen and firm. The top may be covered with a piece of greaseproof paper if it browns too quickly.

DUNDEE CAKE

8 oz. flour
6 oz. butter
6 oz. castor sugar
1 teaspoon baking powder
2 tablespoons ground almonds
4 eggs
6 oz. currants
6 oz. sultanas
2 oz. glacé cherries

2 oz. mixed peel
Grated rind and juice of ½ lemon
1 tablespoon brandy or rum
Pinch salt
1 oz. blanched almonds for top of cake

Glaze
2 tablespoons milk
1 tablespoon sugar

Grease an 8-inch round cake tin and line with
greased greaseproof paper. Prepare the fruit.
Cream the butter and sugar together until the
mixture is white and fluffy. Beat in the eggs, one
at a time, adding a little flour to prevent curdling.
Stir in the ground almonds, fruit, mixed peel,
grated lemon rind and lemon juice. Sift the flour

and baking powder and pinch of salt-together. Fold into the cake mixture. Stir in the brandy or rum. Turn into the cake tin cover with foil and bake in a moderate oven (300°F. 149°C. gas mark 2) for about 2½ hours. Half way through the cooking time, remove the foil and scatter the almonds on top. When the cake is cooked, a skewer or needle inserted into the cake comes out clean.

To Glaze: When the cake is nearly cooked dissolve the tablespoon of sugar in the milk and brush the top of the cake. Allow the cake to cool in the tin. If preferred, the rum or brandy may be poured over the base of the cake after it is cooked. The cake may be kept for months in a tin.

AYRSHIRE SHORTBREAD

4 oz. flour ⎱ or 7 oz. flour	3 oz. castor sugar
4 oz. rice ⎰ 1 oz. cornflour	1 egg yolk
4 oz. butter	1 teaspoon cream

Sieve the flours together and lightly rub in the butter. Stir in the sugar. Bind the mixture together with the beaten egg yolk and the cream. Turn onto a floured board. Divide in half and press out into two rounds. Lightly roll out the rounds to a thickness of ½ inch. Crimp the edges and mark each round into 6-8 sections. Prick with a fork and cook in the centre of a cool oven (300°F. 149°C. gas mark 2) for 45 minutes until firm and browned. Cool on a wire rack and dredge with castor sugar. Break into pieces. Alternatively the mixture may be rolled into two rectangles and marked in strips.

BROONIE

4 oz. flour
5 oz. medium oatmeal
2 oz. butter

3 oz. sugar
1 teaspoon bicarbonate of soda
1 teaspoon ground ginger

2 tablespoons black treacle
1 egg
$\frac{1}{3}$ pint sourmilk or buttermilk

Sift the flour, bicarbonate of soda and ginger
together. Add the oatmeal. Rub in the fat
until the mixture looks like breadcrumbs.
Melt the treacle. Stir into the flour
mixture together with the sugar and egg. Add
enough sour milk or buttermilk to make the
mixture just soft enough to drop from a spoon.
Turn into a greased tin and bake in a moderate
oven (325°F 163°C. gas mark 3) for 1-1½ hours
until firm and well risen. Cool on a wire tray.

EDINBURGH GINGERBREAD

1 lb. flour
1 teaspoon baking powder
¼ teaspoon salt
1 teaspoon ground ginger
1 teaspoon cinnamon
1 teaspoon mixed spice
½ teaspoon ground cloves
8 oz. dates

4 oz. walnuts
6 oz. butter
6 oz. black treacle
8 oz. brown sugar
2 eggs
¼ pint milk
Preserved ginger

Grease a 7 inch square tin and line with greased greaseproof paper. Sift the flour baking powder, salt and spices together. Stone and chop up the dates. Shell and chop up the walnuts. Add the dates and walnuts to the flour mixture. Warm the treacle, sugar and butter together. Whisk the eggs lightly. Add the treacle mixture and the eggs to the flour mixture. Add enough milk to give a dropping consistency. but the mixture should not be too soft. Pour into the tin and bake in a moderate oven (350°F. 177°C. gas mark 4) for 1½ hours until the gingerbread is firm to the touch. Cool on a wire rack. Cut into squares and decorate with pieces of preserved ginger.

BANNOCK OR OATCAKE

4 oz. oatmeal   Pinch salt   2 tablespoons warm water
Pinch bicarbonate of soda   1 teaspoon bacon fat

Mix the oatmeal, bicarbonate of soda and salt together. Make a well in the middle of the mixture and pour in the melted fat. Add enough water to make a stiff dough. Turn out on a board liberally scattered with oatmeal, knead lightly and then roll out to a ¼ inch thickness. Keep the dough well dusted with oatmeal to stop it sticking. Form into a round using a plate. Sprinkle again with oatmeal and cook on a warmed girdle until the edges begin to curl. Turn and cook the other side. The bannock may be cut into quarters or farls. Another bannock may be prepared while the first is cooking. Dough for more than one bannock cannot be prepared at the same time because the dough stiffens so quickly.

OATMEAL SCONES

6 oz. flour
4 oz. fine oatmeal
½ oz. margarine
½ teaspoon bicarbonate of soda

¾ teaspoon cream of tartar
½ teaspoon sugar
Pinch salt
¼ pint milk

Sieve the flour, salt, bicarbonate of soda, and cream of tartar together. Add the oatmeal. Rub in the margarine and add enough milk to make a soft dough. Turn onto a floured board and knead lightly. Roll out to a thickness of ½ inch and cut into rounds. Place on a baking tray and brush with milk. Cook in a hot oven (450°F. 232°C. gas mark 8) for 10 minutes or bake on a hot girdle.

CRANACHAN OR CREAM CROWDIE

2 oz. pinhead oatmeal
½ pint double cream
1-2 oz. castor sugar
4 oz. raspberries
rum or vanilla

Toast the oatmeal lightly in the oven or in a thick-bottomed frying pan over a gentle heat. Beat the cream until-frothy but not stiff. Sweeten to taste. Mix in the oatmeal and flavour with rum or vanilla. Wash and sieve the raspberries and stir into the cream mixture.

PORRIDGE

For each person:
1¼ oz. oatmeal
1 cup water
Pinch salt

Bring the water to the boil. Let the oatmeal fall into the water in a steady stream from the left hand while stirring the mixture briskly with the right hand using a wooden spoon. Cover and simmer for 20-30 minutes. After 10 minutes, add a pinch of salt. Ladle into cold bowls and serve with cream or fresh milk. Each hot spoonful should be dipped in cold cream or milk before eating. A double boiler, if used, ensures that there is no danger of burning.

DRAMBUIE CREAM TRIFLE

⅓ orange jelly
Sponge fingers or ratafia biscuits
¾ pint milk

3 oz. castor sugar
¾ oz. powdered gelatine
2 eggs

½ pint cream
4 oz. Drambuie

Dissolve the jelly in hot water to make ⅓ pint solution and pour into a mould. When cool and thickened but not set, line the sides of the mould with sponge fingers or ratafia biscuits. Leave to set. Bring the milk to the boil. Beat the eggs and blend with the sugar and gelatine. Pour the milk into the egg mixture and return to the saucepan. Heat gently for 3 minutes stirring all the time but do not boil. Whip the cream and add the Drambuie. When the egg custard is cool but not set, fold in the cream mixture. Pour into the sponge finger lined mould and leave to set in a cool place.

DUNDEE MARMALADE

3 lb. seville oranges   6 lb. preserving or granulated sugar
3 lemons   6 pints water

Wash and scrub the fruit. Cut in half and squeeze out the juice. Tie the pips in a muslin bag. Cut up the orange halves and put into a large preserving pan with the water, the juice of the lemons and the bag of pips. Bring to the boil and heat gently until the peel is soft and the volume of the liquid is reduced by half. Lift out the bag of pips, cool and squeeze dry over the pan. Add the sugar and stir until dissolved. Boil rapidly until setting point is reached (200°F — 222°F. 93°C — 105°C). Skin and pot in hot sterilized jars. Seal.

TODDY

Whisky
Sugar
Hot water

Warm a tumbler with warm water. Empty. Into
the glass put 2 teaspoons sugar and a wine glass of
hot water. Stir until the sugar is dissolved. Add a
wine glass of whisky and stir. Then add another
wine glass of hot water and a further wine glass of
whisky.

BUTTERSCOTCH

1 lb. brown sugar
4 oz. butter
Juice of 1 lemon or
1 teaspoon ground ginger

Heat the sugar in a saucepan until it melts. Cream the butter and add slowly to the sugar. Continue heating and stirring until a little of the mixture hardens when dropped into cold water. Add the lemon juice or ground ginger. Beat quickly with a fork. Pour into a buttered tin and mark into squares. Break into pieces when cold.

INDEX